Earaches

ELAINE LANDAU

mc **Marshall Cavendish**
Benchmark
New York

Published by Marshall Cavendish Benchmark
An imprint of Marshall Cavendish Corporation

This publication represents the opinions and views of the author based on Elaine Landau's personal experience, knowledge, and research. The information in this book serves as a general guide only. The author and publisher have used their best efforts in preparing this book and disclaim liability rising directly and indirectly from the use and application of this book.

Other Marshall Cavendish Offices:
Marshall Cavendish International (Asia) Private Limited, 1 New Industrial Road, Singapore 536196 • Marshall Cavendish International (Thailand) Co Ltd. 253 Asoke, 12th Flr, Sukhumvit 21 Road, Klongtoey Nua, Wattana, Bangkok 10110, Thailand • Marshall Cavendish (Malaysia) Sdn Bhd, Times Subang, Lot 46, Subang Hi-Tech Industrial Park, Batu Tiga, 40000 Shah Alam, Selangor Darul Ehsan, Malaysia

Marshall Cavendish is a trademark of Times Publishing Limited
All websites were available and accurate when this book was sent to press.

Library of Congress Cataloging-in-Publication Data
Landau, Elaine.
Earaches / by Elaine Landau.
p. cm. — (Head-to-toe health)
Includes index.
Summary: "Provides basic information about earaches and their
prevention"—Provided by publisher.
  ISBN 978-0-7614-4831-0
  1. Earache in children—Juvenile literature. I. Title.
RF291.5.C45L36 2010
617.8—dc22
2009030909

Editor: Joy Bean
Publisher: Michelle Bisson
Art Director: Anahid Hamparian
Series Designer: Alex Ferrari

Photo research by Candlepants Incorporated
Cover Photo: Shutterstock
The photographs in this book are used by permission and through the courtesy of:
Alamy Images: Christina Kennedy, 4; Rob Walls, 17. Getty Images: Steve Lewis, 6; Brian J. Skerry, 7; 3D4Medical.com , 12; Jose Luis Pelaez, 18; Mel Yates, 21; Vanessa Davies, 23; Sean Ellis, 25. Photo Researchers Inc.: VEM, 9; Dr P. Marazzi, 11; Brian Evans, 15. Shutterstock:13.

Printed in Malaysia(T)
1 3 5 6 4 2

CONTENTS

My Ear Hurts!

OUCH! You woke up this morning, and your ear really hurt. It's a throbbing pain. You can't even lie down on that side. You tried to eat breakfast, but chewing made it feel even worse. So did sipping through a straw. You've got an earache, and it's just awful!

Lots of kids get earaches. Only colds are a more common sickness among young people. Three out of four kids have had an earache by the time they are three years old. So if you get an earache, one thing is certain. You are not alone.

EARS ARE IMPORTANT

Bet you don't spend lots of time thinking about your ears. Before you get an earache, you may not think about them at all. Your ears are simply those floppy, cup-shaped things on the sides of your head. Yet your ears let you hear, and hearing connects you to the world in important ways.

◄ **When you have an earache, even touching your ear can hurt.**

Dogs have better hearing than people. They can hear sounds at both a lower pitch and a much higher pitch than people.

Your life would be very different if you couldn't hear. Imagine not hearing your friends on the phone or the teacher in class. You would not hear your favorite music or even the sound of an alarm clock or doorbell. Of course, you wouldn't hear your mom yelling at you either—but you might miss that after a while.

SAFE AND SOUND

Your hearing also helps keep you safe. Without it, you'd miss the sound of a smoke alarm warning you of a fire.

Your hearing is important. That's why you should know as much as you can about your ears.

EARS HERE

Look at your head in the mirror. It's hard to
miss your ears. Yet some animals have ears you can't see.
The harp seal does not have ears on the outside. It just has two small
ear openings on the sides of its head. Harp seals hear quite
well but are often called earless seals.

How Did This Happen to Me?

Earaches can be very painful. No one wants one. So if you get one, you might wonder, "Why is this happening to me?"

Earaches can happen in more than one way. Sometimes an ear injury causes the pain. Ever see little kids stick things into their ears? That's a dangerous way to play. Sometimes older kids—and even adults—stick things in their ears to clean them. That's another bad idea.

Poking around in your ear can lead to trouble. You can damage your eardrum, and that can give you a very painful earache. It can also result in hearing loss and other problems. Yet most earaches are not caused by injuries. Earaches usually result from ear **infections**. Infections start when germs find their way into your body and multiply. In this case, germs in your ear are causing the problem. Let's take a closer look at the ear to see how this happens.

YOUR EAR—INSIDE AND OUT

The part of the ear you see is your outer ear, or **pinna**. But there's a lot more to your ear. From the outer ear an ear canal leads to a slim membrane known as the eardrum. Your eardrum separates your outer ear from your middle ear.

Your middle ear is very small. It's about the size of a wrinkly raisin. Yet it still contains three tiny bones called the hammer, anvil, and stirrup. These bones link the eardrum to the inner ear. Your middle ear is also connected to the back of your nose and throat through a small tube. This passageway is known as the **Eustachian tube**. This tube allows fluid to drain from your middle ear into your throat.

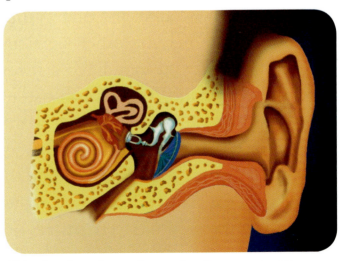

This drawing shows the parts of your ear you don't see.

WHEN TROUBLE STARTS

Usually your Eustachian tube works just fine. But things can change when you have a cold or allergy. That's when your nose may produce lots of a thick fluid called **mucus**. This can cause your Eustachian tube to become swollen and blocked. Then the fluid in your middle ear can't drain out.

Germs, such as **bacteria** and **viruses**, travel up the Eustachian tubes from your throat. They multiply in the fluid. The trapped fluid causes pressure to build up in your ear. The fluid pushes on your eardrum, and that hurts. POW! You've got an earache!

An earache is often just one **symptom,** or sign, of an ear infection. There may be other signs as well. When you have an ear infection, you may have a fever or feel dizzy. You may be cranky, too, and not want to eat anything. Sometimes, you can't hear as well while your ear is infected. The sounds aren't as loud or clear as they usually are.

Although rare, you may even find that fluid is leaking out of the infected ear. This happens when the pressure from the trapped fluid causes the eardrum to **rupture,** or burst. At that point, some of the fluid drains out. In some cases a torn eardrum will heal on its own. Other times, a doctor has to surgically repair it.

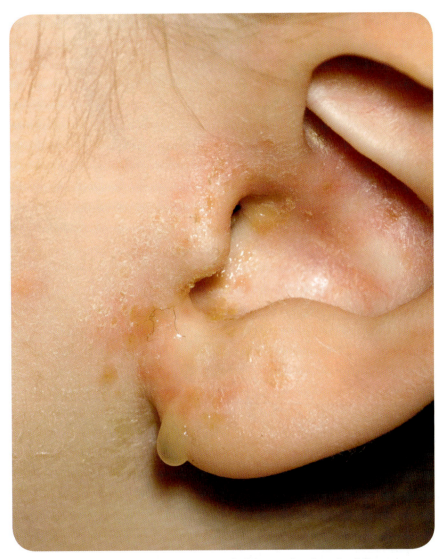

In rare cases of an ear infection, fluid can leak out of the ear.

ITTY BITTY TROUBLEMAKERS

The bacteria and viruses that cause ear infections are tiny troublemakers. You can't see them with the naked eye. Bacteria must be magnified with a microscope a thousand times to be seen. Viruses are even smaller. They are among the smallest germs on the planet. Billions of viruses could fit on the period at the end of this sentence. Now that's really small!

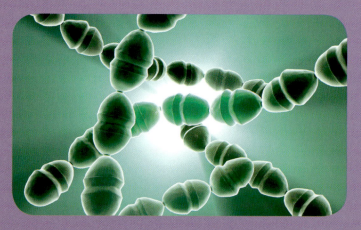

GETTING AN EARACHE

See if you can answer this TRUE or FALSE question correctly: Can you catch an earache from someone sitting next to you at school?

The answer is FALSE.

You can't catch an earache from another person. But you can catch colds from people around you. A cold can sometimes lead to an ear infection, and an ear infection can give you an earache.

LITTLE KIDS, BIG PROBLEMS

Guess who gets more earaches—kids or grown-ups? If you said kids, you're right. Children under the age of ten get three-quarters

Young children get more earaches than both teens and adults.

of all ear infections. Very young children get them more often than older children.

There's a reason for this. In adults and older children the Eustachian tubes are in a nearly straight up and down position. Fluid easily drains out of them.

Younger children have smaller and shorter Eustachian tubes. Their tubes slant almost sideways. This makes it harder for fluid to drain out. Germs can easily grow in the trapped fluid.

ANOTHER KIND OF EARACHE

Most ear infections occur in the middle ear. But you can also get an infection in your outer ear. This happens when bacteria grow in the ear canal. The ear canal leads from the outer ear to the eardrum. If your ear canal becomes infected, you'll know it. Just touching the outside of your ear will hurt. Yikes!

HOW DOES IT HAPPEN?

Usually a layer of sticky yellow earwax protects the ear canal. It allows water to easily flow into and out of your ears when you shower or swim.

But sometimes things go wrong. Let's say you've been swimming a lot. All that water can wash away your earwax.

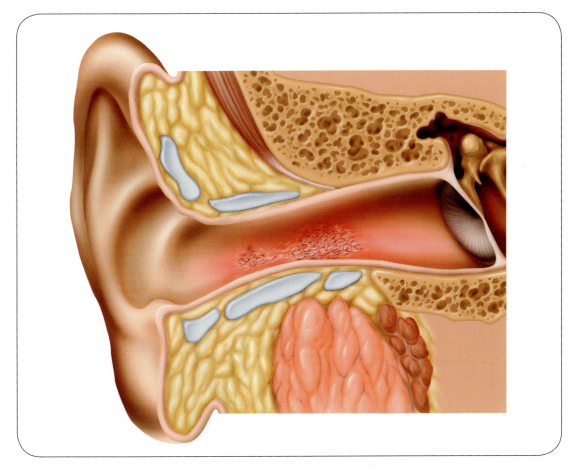

This illustration shows an infected ear canal.

Now water more easily remains in your ear. That fluid acts as a breeding ground for germs. Before you know, it you've got an ear infection.

These infections are sometimes called swimmer's ear. Yet you don't have to be a swimmer to get one. A scratch on your ear canal can become infected as well. This can give you a painful earache too.

THE SCOOP ON EARWAX

Think earwax is just about the yuckiest stuff on the planet? Think again. That icky, sticky yellow goop doesn't just protect you when you swim. It also traps dirt that can blow into your ears. The same goes for tiny insects that may fly or crawl into your ears as well.

EAR PIERCING PROBLEM

So far, we've talked about ear infections in the middle and outer ear. But what if you pierce your ears? Your earlobes can become infected too. You may have pierced your ears to look good. Yet an infected earlobe looks and feels just awful.

The infected earlobe often becomes swollen and red. A thick, yellowish fluid called **pus** may ooze from the pierced hole. Your whole earlobe can feel quite sore. Just touching it may hurt.

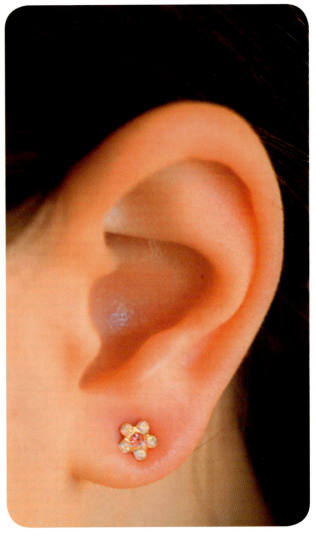

Notice how red this girl's earlobe is around her earring. Her newly pierced ears may be infected.

GETTING HELP

What should you do if:

Your ear aches and feels sort of stuffed up.

You don't think you're hearing as well as you usually do.

You're feverish and don't feel like eating.

It sounds like you have all the symptoms of an ear infection. You need to see a doctor!

AT THE DOCTOR'S OFFICE

The doctor will look into your ear with a small special flashlight called an **otoscope**. It's important to see if your eardrum is red and bulging out. If it is, you probably have an ear

A doctor examines a young girl's ears. These examinations are painless.

infection. Doctors also sometimes use the otoscope to blow a small puff of air into your ear. This will show if your eardrum is moving the way it should.

YUP, IT'S AN EAR INFECTION

Your doctor may not treat your ear infection right away. Some doctors like to wait a day or two after seeing their patients. They want to see if the body can defeat the infection on its own. This is known as the WASP (wait-and-see period).

Other times the doctor may give you an **antibiotic** that day. Antibiotics are drugs often used to treat ear infections. They kill the bacteria that caused the infection. However, antibiotics will not work if a virus caused your ear infection.

If you are given an antibiotic, it's important to take it for as long as your doctor tells you to. It doesn't matter if your ear feels better after a day or two. If you don't finish all the medicine, the pain could come back again. That means the infection is back as well.

Earaches Aren't Welcome Here

Sometimes you can't help getting an earache. It just happens. But there are things you can do to try to get fewer earaches. Put these helpful hints to work for you.

TENDER TREATMENT, PLEASE

Don't stick things in your ears. Don't do it to be funny. Don't do it to clean your ears either. It's just asking for

Sticking anything in your ear is a really bad idea. The boy in the picture won't be smiling if he damages his ear.

trouble. Straws, pencils, cotton swabs, and safety pins should never enter your ears.

IT'S SWELL TO STAY WELL

At times, having a cold can lead to an ear infection. So it's important to try to stay well. Often, cold germs are spread through touch. You can have germs on your hands and not even know it.

Do your best to get rid of germs. Wash your hands when you come home from school and after coming in from playing outdoors. You should also wash your hands before you eat and after going to the bathroom. Try not to touch your eyes, nose, or mouth before washing your hands. That's how germs can get inside your body.

Most people don't spend enough time washing their hands. Do you? You should be able to sing the "Happy Birthday" song twice before starting to rinse.

Like colds, allergies can also lead to ear infections. If you're supposed to take medicine regularly for an allergy, be sure you do so. Try to stay away from whatever you're allergic to as well. This isn't always easy. If you're allergic to something like dust, it's just about everywhere. But keeping your room clean can help a bit.

Always use soap when washing your hands. Water alone will not do the job.

SWIMMER'S EAR NOT WANTED HERE

Do you swim a lot? That doesn't mean you have to get swimmer's ear. There are ways to guard against it.

Try wearing earplugs in the water. When you come out of the water, dry your ears well. Whoever takes care of you can also get some special drops at the drug store. A few of these drops placed in your ears will get rid of any wetness there.

AVOID PIERCED EAR PROBLEMS

What if you've just pierced your ears? To avoid infections, you've got to keep your earlobes very clean. Wash your hands well before touching your ears.

You should clean your earlobes daily for about a week after the piercing. This can be done with an antibiotic cream from the drug store or some rubbing alcohol on a cotton ball. Either should be applied to your earlobes to kill any germs hanging out there.

It's okay to gently move your earrings around to clean your earlobes. Just don't take out your earrings until the pierced holes are fully healed. If you do, the holes can close up. Having to have your ears pierced again is no fun for anyone.

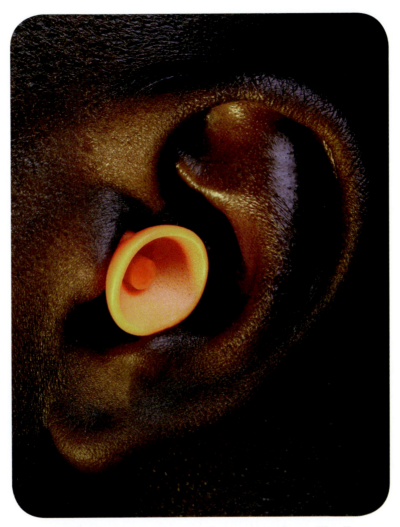

It's a good idea for swimmers to use earplugs, like the one seen here, in the water.

I DID EVERYTHING I SHOULD, AND I STILL GOT AN EARACHE

What if you get an earache anyway? Don't panic, but don't keep it a secret either. Tell whoever takes care of you what's wrong.

With proper medical care, you'll feel better soon. But if left untreated, your ear infection could become more serious. In some cases, middle and outer ear infections have led to permanent hearing loss. Never ignore ear pain. Your ears serve you well. Keep them in tip-top shape.

DID YOU KNOW?

Being around cigarette smoke could increase your chances of getting an ear infection. This is especially true during the first three years of life. Studies show that being near cigarette smoke then nearly doubles your risk of having frequent ear infections.

GLOSSARY

antibiotic — a drug used to kill harmful bacteria in the body

bacteria — germs that cannot be seen without a microscope. Not all bacteria are harmful. Some forms of bacteria are helpful and even necessary

Eustachian tube — a small tube connecting the middle ear to the back of the nose and throat

infection — an illness caused by bacteria or viruses

mucus — a sticky substance produced by the body to protect it

otoscope — a small, special flashlight used by doctors to see into the ear

pinna — the part of the ear that is outside the head

pus — a thick, yellowish liquid that comes out of an infected area

rupture — to burst or break open

symptom — an outward sign of an illness

virus — a kind of tiny germ too small to be seen without a special microscope. Viruses are even smaller than bacteria

FIND OUT MORE

BOOKS

Gray, Susan Heinrichs. *The Ears*. Mankato, MN: Child's World, 2005.

Landau, Elaine. *The Sense of Hearing*. New York: Children's Press, 2008.

Olien, Rebecca. *Hearing*. Mankato, MN: Capstone Press, 2005.

Schuette, Sarah L. *Taking Care of My Ears*. Mankato, MN: Capstone Press, 2005.

Schuh, Mari C. *The Sense of Hearing*. Minneapolis, MN: Bellwether Media, 2007.

Verdick, Elizabeth. *Germs Are Not For Sharing*. Minneapolis: Free Spirit Publishing, 2006.

DVDS

All About Health and Hygiene (The Human Body for Children) Schlessinger Media, 2006.

All About the Senses (The Human Body for Children) Schlessinger
    Media, 2006.

Healthy Habits 101…Teaching Kids to Stay Healthy for Life, Big Kids
    Productions, Inc., 2008.

WEB SITES

How Does the Ear Work?

www.helpkidshear.org/resources/starter/ear.htm

This easy-to-understand website will help you learn about the different
parts of the ear and how they work together.

Meet the Scrub Club

www.scrubclub.org

Learn how to combat germ villains through the fun games on this
website.

What Is an Ear Infection?

http://kidshealth.org/kid/ill_injure/sick/ear_infection.html

This is a great website for learning more about ear infections and how
you can avoid them.

INDEX

Page numbers in **boldface** are illustrations.

About the Author

The award-winning author Elaine Landau has written more than three hundred books for young readers. Many of these are on health and science topics.

Landau received a bachelor's degree in English and journalism from New York University and a master's degree in library and information science from Pratt Institute. You can visit Elaine Landau at her website: www.elainelandau.com.